1(

School
Jokes for Kids

I.P. Grinning
&
I.P. Factly

To Gilly.

1.

Why did the teacher get stronger bulbs for the school room?

Because the class was a little dim!

2.

Who's the king of your desk?

Your ruler!

3.

Why did the sun not bother going to college?

It already had a million degrees!

4.

History teacher: How did the Dark Ages get their name?

Pupil: From all the Knights!

5.

History teacher: How did Vikings communicate?

Pupil: Norse code!

6.

Headmaster: Why are your eyes crossed?

Teacher: I just can't control my pupils!

7.

History teacher: Why is England so wet?

Pupil: Because Kings and Queens have reigned there for centuries!

8.

Why did the music teacher get locked in his piano?

The keys were stuck on the outside!

9.

Teacher: Where might you find the English Channel?

Pupil: I don't know, is it near the MTV channel?

10.

What class does a butterfly like best?

Mothematics!

11.

Why do music teachers need stepladders?

To reach the high notes!

12.

Mother: How did you find school?

Son: It was there when I got off the bus!

13.

What's the worst thing ever found in a school cafeteria?

The Food!

14.

What kind of plates do Martians use at school?

Flying saucers!

15.

How can you guarantee straight A's?

Use a ruler!

16.

Why do noses hate going to school?

They are always getting picked on!

17.

Mother: How did you manage to get told off so many times today?

Son: I'm an early riser!

18.

History teacher: Who was the biggest knight at King Arthur's round table?

Pupil: Sir Cumference!

19.

Teacher: How do you get a higher education?

Pupil: Study on top of a mountain!

20.

Why are librarians good at fishing?

They've always got lots of bookworms to use as bait!

21.

Mother: How was your new teacher?

Son: Not good, she wanted to know how to spell cat!

22.

Why do librarians often talk about silent vegetables?

Because they are always saying "Quiet peas"!

23.

Why did the boy run into school 20 minutes late?

Because he had been told not to stroll into school 20 minutes late again!

24.

Where do music teachers go to find new pianos?

Florida Keys!

25.

Why did the teacher describe the boy's test results as underwater?

Because they were below 'C' level!

26.

Where do schools get their pens and pencils?

Pennsylvania!

27.

If I gave you fifty dollars and your father gave you another fifty what would you have?

A new bike!

28.

Headmaster: Why did you pass everything except history class?

Pupil: I didn't take history!

29.

Math Teacher: If I lay one egg here, three over here and then two more here, how many eggs will there be?

Pupil: None! You can't lay eggs!

30.

Geography teacher: What is the capital of France?

Pupil: F!

31.

History Teacher: What did William Tell's son say when the apple on his head was hit?

Pupil: That was an arrow escape!

32.

Geography teacher: Which country is known to be fast moving?

Pupil: Rusha!

33.

Teacher: How did Noah keep the ark illuminated?

Pupil: Floodlights!

34.

History Teacher: Why did Henry the eighth get through so many wives?

Pupil: He chopped and changed a lot!

35.

History Teacher: What would people have worn at the Boston Tea Party?

Party Hats!

36.

History teacher: What happened at the Boston Tea Party?

Annoyed pupil: I don't know - they didn't invite me!

37.

What's purple or green and can be seen from space?

The grape wall of China!

38.

History teacher: How did Romans greet their leaders when the weather was bad?

Pupil: Hail Caesar!

39.

Teacher: Who built the ark and saved the animals?

Pupil: I have No-ah idea!

40.

History teacher: Where was the Declaration of Independence signed?

Pupil: At the bottom!

41.

Teacher: What do Alexander the Great and Kermit the Frog have in common?

Pupil: Middle names!

42.

History teacher: Who cut the Roman Empire in half?

Pupil: A pair of Caesars!

43.

Geography teacher: Where are elephants found?

Pupil: In lost luggage!

44.

What kind of sum does a pupil like best?

Sum-mer!

45.

Teacher: Where is the best place to learn multiplication?

Pupil: On tables!

46.

Pupil: Why are you wearing sunglasses?

Teacher: Because you are all so bright!

47.

Teacher: Why did you miss school yesterday?

Pupil: I didn't, there's was plenty of things to do at home!

48.

Pupil: Why are you dipping your toes in the swimming pool Miss?

Teacher: I'm testing the water!

49.

Teacher: What would I have if I had 2 melons in this hand and 6 bananas in the other hand?

Pupil: Big hands!

50.

Teacher: What is the shortest month?

Pupil: May - with only three letters!

51.

Why do some teachers draw on windows?

To make the lesson clear!

52.

How do bees get to their lessons in a morning?

School buzz!

53.

What is special about the Mississippi river?

It has four eyes but can't see a thing!

54.

What is the name of the little rivers that flow into the Nile?

Juve-niles!

I.P. Grinning

55.

Geography teacher: Where are the Andes?

Pupil: At the end of my sleevies!

56.

Why did Eve decide to go to New York?

She wanted a taste of the Big Apple!

57.

Geography teacher: Can you name the Poles?

Pupil: Yes, North, South and tad...!

58.

What meals do math teachers enjoy?

Square meals!

59.

Science teacher: How do we deal with crude oil?

Pupil: Send it to the headmaster!

60.

Teacher: How did Noah manage to design an ark?

Pupil: He was an ark-itect!

61.

History teacher: Where did the Pilgrims land when they got off the Mayflower?

Pupil: On the shore!

62.

History teacher: Where is Hadrian's Wall?

Pupil: Around his house!

63.

History teacher: Why does history repeat itself?

Pupil: Because no-one listens in history lessons!

64.

History teacher: Who came after the first President of the USA?

Pupil: The second President!

65.

Why did Noah never catch many fish?

He only had two worms!

66.

History Teacher: When was Rome built?

Pupil: At night - because Rome was not built in a day!

67.

Why are math books usually blue?

Because they have so many problems!

68.

History Teacher: What was King Arthur's Camelot?

Pupil: A place for the knights to park their camels!

69.

History Teacher: What was written on the headstones of knight's graves?

Pupil: Rust in peace!

70.

History teacher: Why did the dinosaurs go extinct?

Pupil: I don't know, that's more your era than mine!

71.

What famous commander invented fireplaces?

Alexander the grate!

72.

What happened when the horse walked into the classroom?

The teacher asked, "Why the long face?"!

73.

History Teacher: Why did Robin Hood rob the rich?

Pupil: The poor had nothing worth stealing!

74.

History teacher: Who invented fractions?

Pupil: Henry the 1/8th!

75.

History Teacher: Where did warriors in the middle ages learn to fight?

Pupil: At knight school!

76.

Geography teacher: What do you know about the Dead Sea?

Confused pupil: I didn't even know it was sick!

77.

History Teacher: When were the Pharaohs buried in pyramids?

Pupil: When they were dead!

78.

Geography teacher: What did Delaware...?

Pupil: A New Jersey!

79.

Pupil: What is your favorite rock group Miss?

Geography teacher: The Blue Ridge Mountains!

80.

Why are rabbits so good at math?

They are the quickest multipliers!

81.

Teacher: What would you have if you took home three dogs today and five tomorrow?

Pupil: A very angry mom!

82.

Teacher: What would you get if you add 342 and 286 and then multiply by 6?

Pupil: The wrong answer!

83.

What is a math teacher's favorite tree?

Geometr-ee!

84.

What kind of pliers might you need in a math lesson?

Multi-pliers!

85.

Teacher: Where are the Great Plains?

Pupil: In the airport!

86.

What would you have if you had an apple, an orange, a banana and five grapes?

A small fruit salad!

87.

Why was the library so tall?

It had lots of stories!

88.

Teacher: Who can include the word 'politics' in a sentence?

Pupil: After the parrot ate my watch Polly-tics!

89.

Teacher: Who can include the word *'ambush'* in a sentence?

Pupil: I plucked some lovely ham from the *'am bush*!

90.

What is the best state to go to school?

Alabama - you are guaranteed four A's and one B!

91.

Math teacher: Do you need a pocket calculator?

Pupil: No, it's not pockets I'm struggling to count!

92.

Teacher: Who can include the word '*lettuce*' in a sentence?

Pupil: Can you *lettuce* go home now?

93.

Teacher: Who knows who broke the sound barrier?

Pupil: Johnny was playing with it last!

94.

Teacher: What's a mushroom?

Pupil: Another name for the school canteen!

95.

Why are school cooks so evil?

They beat eggs and whip cream!

96.

What is the first thing elves learn at school?

The elf-abet!

97.

Teacher: I hope I haven't just seen you copying from Johnny's test!

Pupil: I hope so too!

98.

Pupil: How did you know I copied from Johnny?

Teacher: For question 12 he wrote, "Don't know" and you wrote, "Me neither"!

99.

Teacher: What are you going to be when you leave school?

Pupil: Old!

100.

Mother: You got a terrible mark, why do you think your teacher likes you?

Son: All those kisses she wrote on my test!

101.

Teacher: Why are you doing cartwheels in my class?

Pupil: I'm turning things over in my mind!

ABOUT THE AUTHOR

IP Factly is the happy father of 8 and 10 year old boys. Their hilariously awful attempts to make up their own jokes inspired the IP Factly series of joke books for kids.

Hopefully you'll enjoy this book as much as he enjoyed writing it.

Printed in Poland
by Amazon Fulfillment
Poland Sp. z o.o., Wrocław